Materials
Plastic

Chris Oxlade

www.heinemann.co.uk/library
Visit our website to find out more information about Heinemann Library books.

To Order:

 Phone 44 (0) 1865 888066

 Send a fax to 44 (0) 1865 314091

Visit the Heinemann Library Bookshop at www.heinemann.co.uk/library to browse our catalogue and order online.

First published in Great Britain by Heinemann Library, Halley Court, Jordan Hill, Oxford OX2 8EJ, a division of Reed Educational and Professional Publishing Ltd.
Heinemann is a registered trademark of Reed Educational and Professional Publishing Ltd.

OXFORD MELBOURNE AUCKLAND JOHANNESBURG BLANTYRE
GABORONE IBADAN PORTSMOUTH (NH) USA CHICAGO

Designed by Storeybooks
Originated by Dot Gradations Ltd
Printed by South China Printing in Hong Kong/China

ISBN 0 431 03741 8 (hardback)   ISBN 0 431 03746 9 (paperback)
06 05 04 03 02   06 05 04 03 02
10 9 8 7 6 5 4 3 2 1   10 9 8 7 6 5 4 3 2 1

British Library Cataloguing in Publication Data
        Oxlade, Chris
        Plastic. – (Materials)
        1. Plastic
        I. Title
        620.1'923

Acknowledgements
Barnaby's Picture Library /H. K. Maitland p.19; Corbis pp.24, /Bob Krist p.4, Image Bank p.11; Kate Bryant-Mole p.16; Noel Whittal p.29; Oxford Scientific Films/Edward Parker p.26; Photodisc p.14; PPL Library p.15; Science Photo Library p. 27; Shell Library pp.17, 22; Stone p.12; Tudor Photography pp.5, 6, 7, 8, 9, 10, 13, 18, 20, 23, 25.

Cover photograph reproduced with permission of Tudor Photography.

Every effort has been made to contact copyright holders of any material reproduced in this book. Any omissions will be rectified in subsequent printings if notice is given to the publishers.

Contents

You can find words shown in bold, **like this**, in the glossary.

What is plastic?

New plastic things are made from these plastic beads.

The word 'plastic' comes from the Greek word '*plastikos*' which means 'formable'.

plastic beads

Plastic is a man-made material. It is made in factories from **chemicals**. These plastic beads have just been **manufactured**. They will be made into plastic things.

4

Plastic is an important material. People make many different things from it.

Did you know that there are more than 50 different types of plastic and that more are being developed all the time?

These objects are all made from plastic.

boxes

skittles

spade

bucket

beakers

comb

pegs

balls

Hard and soft plastics

rubb
bin

Hard plastic is a good material for a rubbish bin, because it is strong but light and waterproof.

Some plastics are very hard. Hard plastics can be very strong. They may be **brittle**. They do not stretch or bend. When brittle plastics are stretched or bent, they may snap in two.

Some plastics are very soft and **flexible**. They are easy to stretch or bend. When soft plastic is stretched a lot, it does not go back into shape afterwards.

Hosepipes are made of flexible plastic that bends easily.

hosepipe

7

Hot and cold plastics

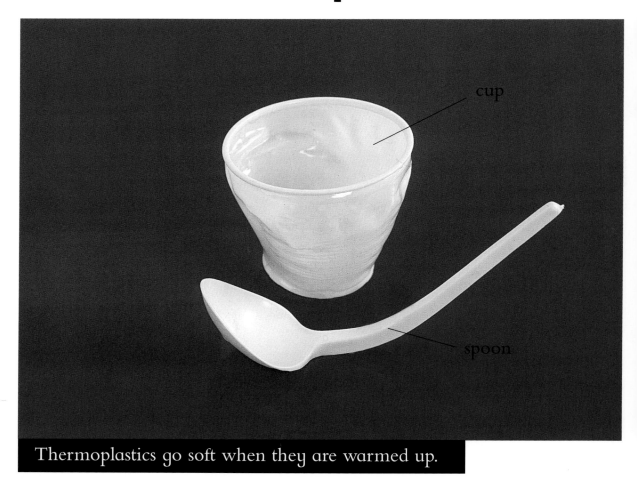

cup

spoon

Thermoplastics go soft when they are warmed up.

There are two different families of plastics. The plastics in one family go soft when they are warmed up. They go hard again when they cool down. These are called thermoplastics.

The plastics in the other family do not go soft when they are warmed up. They stay hard instead. These are called thermosetting plastics.

At some stage while they are being made, all plastics are liquid and can be shaped.

Thermosetting plastics stay hard when they are warmed.

plastic container

Waterproof plastics

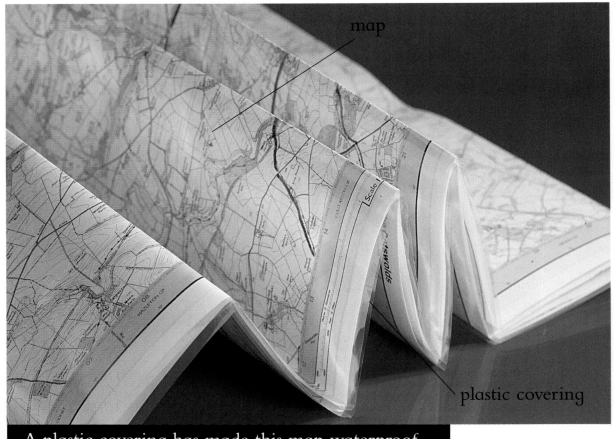

map

plastic covering

A plastic covering has made this map waterproof.

All kinds of plastic are waterproof. They don't let water through and water does not soak into them. You can make paper or card waterproof by covering them with plastic.

Because plastics are waterproof, they last for a very long time. They don't rot away like wood, and they don't **rust** like **steel**, even if they are left outside.

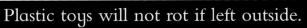
Plastic toys will not rot if left outside.

— plastic slide

Plastics are less expensive than other materials.

Electricity and heat

Plastics don't let **electricity** pass through them. They are called electrical **insulators**. Telephone wires that carry electricity are covered in plastic. This stops the electricity flowing to other wires.

John Wesley Hyatt, an American printer and inventor, made the first plastic in 1869. He invented a type of plastic called celluloid.

plastic casing

The cable has a plastic casing.

Some drinking cups are made from a plastic called **expanded** polystyrene which is full of air bubbles. It does not let heat pass through it. It stops the heat from burning your hands.

Expanded polystyrene is also used in insulation and ceiling tiles.

This cup is made from expanded polystyrene.

polystyrene cup

Making plastics

oil rig

Oil rigs like this one pump oil from the sea-bed.

Plastics are made in factories from **chemicals**.
Most of the chemicals come from **oil** found
underground or under the sea. Different plastics
are made by mixing different chemicals together.

Some plastics are made just before they are used. The plastic for this boat **hull** was made by mixing two liquids together. After a few minutes, the plastic became hard.

The plastic used for this hull has only just been made.

hull

boat-builder

This hull is made of plastic and glass. It is very strong.

Shaping plastics

moulded plastic

This bath toy has been made from moulded plastic.

Many plastic objects, or things, are made in a **mould**. Hot, **molten** plastic is poured into the mould. When the plastic has gone hard again, the new object is taken out of the mould.

Long, thin plastic objects are made by pushing hot, molten plastic through a hole. This is called extrusion. Plastic pipes and **fibres** are made like this.

pipes

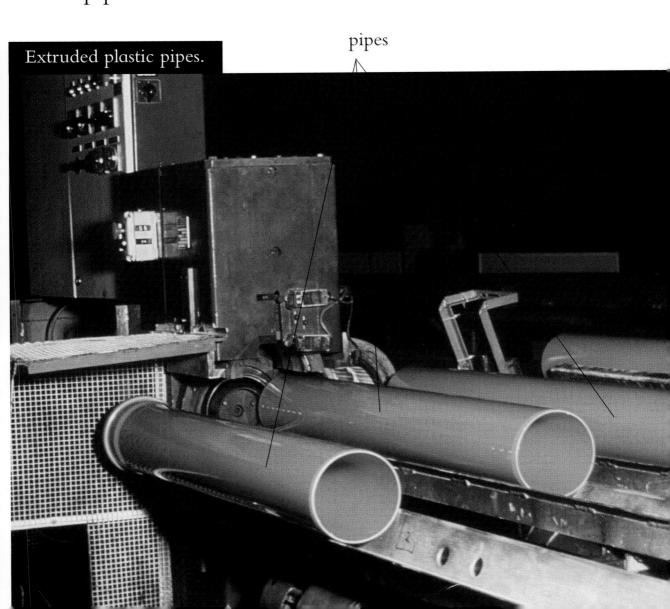

Extruded plastic pipes.

Bottles and tubes

bottle · box · jug · beaker · bowl

Plastic makes useful containers.

Do you have any of these plastic containers at home?

Plastic is often used instead of glass to make bottles. Plastic bottles do not smash if they fall, and are lighter to carry than glass ones.

Plastic pipes and tubes carry liquids and gases. These strong plastic pipes are being laid underground. They carry gas for cooking and heating.

> Different coloured plastic pipes are used for different things. These yellow pipes are used for carrying gas.

This plastic gas pipe will last longer than a metal one.

gas pipe

Plastic packaging

Plastic wrappings keep food fresh.

shopping bag

plastic bag

shrink-wrapped fruit

Thin sheets of plastic are used to make shopping bags and wrapping for foods. Some plastics are wrapped around objects and then heated up to make them shrink.

Expanded polystyrene is a kind of plastic. It is a strong, light material often used for packaging. It is full of tiny air bubbles.

expanded polystyrene

Expanded polystyrene protects things from bumps and scrapes.

Plastic fibres and fabrics

nylon fibres

These fibres are made of a plastic called nylon.

An American called Wallace Hume Carothers helped develop several plastics, including nylon.

A **fibre** is a thin strand of material, such as a hair. Plastic fibres are made by pushing hot, **molten** plastic through tiny holes.

Fleece jackets are usually made from recycled plastic!

fleece

Fleece jackets are made with plastic fibres.

A fabric is made by joining fibres together. Fabrics like fleece are made with plastic fibres. They last a long time and don't go baggy.

Building with plastic

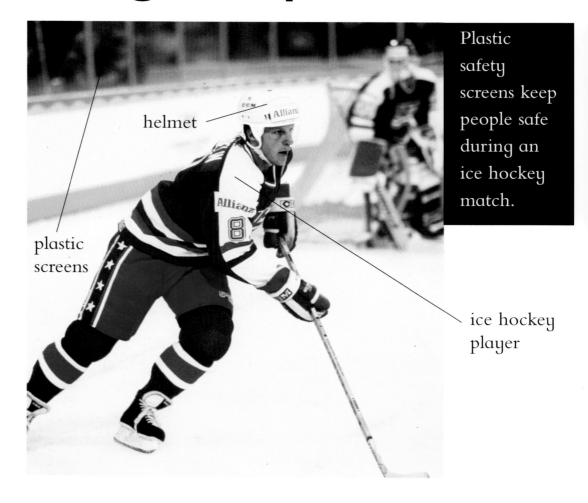

helmet

plastic screens

Plastic safety screens keep people safe during an ice hockey match.

ice hockey player

Builders often use plastics instead of other materials. These screens are made of hard, see-through plastic. They don't shatter if people run into them.

Window frames, doors, gutters and pipes are made from a plastic called PVC. This lasts a long time. It is strong and waterproof, and does not need to be painted like wood or metal.

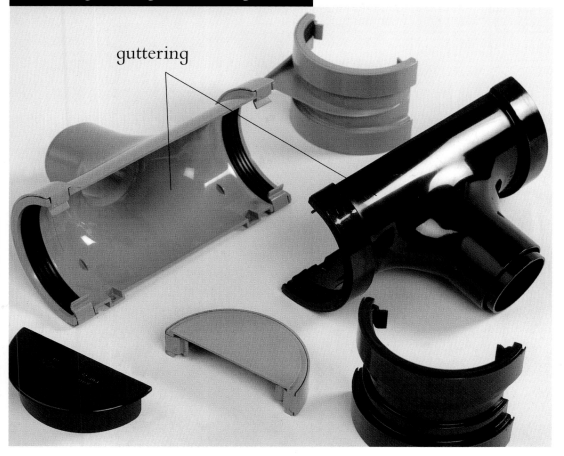

Plastic guttering lasts a long time.

guttering

Recycling plastics

Plastic is a useful material because some plastic does not rot or is very, very slow to rot. This can cause problems. When we throw away plastic things, they may last for ever. There is then too much rubbish.

Plastic rubbish can be hard to get rid of.

plastic waste

Some new plastics break down when they are left in sunlight.

Plastic can be recycled to make new things.

plastic waste

Some plastic things, such as bottles, can be collected and **recycled**. They are melted down to make plastic beads and then made into new things.

Do you remember what plastic beads look like? Turn to page 4 to see if you were right.

Fact file

▶ Plastic is a man-made, or **synthetic**, material. It is not a **natural** material. It is made in factories from **chemicals** made from **oil**.

▶ Some kinds of plastic are hard and difficult to stretch. Some kinds are soft and easy to stretch.

▶ Some kinds of plastic go soft when they are heated. Other kinds of plastic stay hard.

▶ Plastics are waterproof. Many plastics do not rot away.

▶ **Electricity** and heat do not flow through plastics.

▶ Plastics are not attracted by **magnets**.

Would you believe it?

A plastic called Kevlar is stronger than the metal **steel**, but weighs less than steel. You could hang on a Kevlar **fibre** as thin as the lead inside a pencil. This person is hanging on Kevlar fibres.

Kevlar fibres are very strong yet very thin.

parachute

Kevlar fibres

Glossary

a
b
c
d
e
f
g
h
i
j
k
l
m
n
o
p
q
r
s
t
u
v
w
x
y
z

brittle snaps or breaks when it is bent, stretched or dropped on a hard surface

chemicals materials that are used in factories and homes to do many jobs, including cleaning and protecting

electricity form of energy. We use electricity to make electric machines work.

expanded made bigger

fibre long, thin piece of material, like a hair

hull main part of a boat or ship that sits in the water

insulator material that does not let electricity or heat flow through it

magnet object that attracts iron and steel

manufactured made in a factory

molten solid material that is heated until it melts

mould shape that runny plastic is poured into to make a plastic object

natural comes from plants, animals or the rocks in the earth

oil thick, black liquid found underground or under the sea. We get lots of useful chemicals from oil. Some are used to make plastics. Petrol for cars also comes from oil.

recycle use again instead of throwing away

rust browny-red substance that forms on iron or steel when it is left out in the rain or wet

steel strong, hard metal

synthetic artificially made, not natural

More books to read

Science All Around Me: Materials by Karen Bryant-Mole, Heinemann Library, 1996

Science Files: Plastic by Steve Parker, Heinemann Library, 2001

Shooting Stars: Material Matters by Robert Roland, Belitha Press, 2002

I Can Help Recycle Rubbish by V Smith, Franklin Watts, 2001

Materials: Glass by Chris Oxlade, Heinemann Library, 2002

Index